What Plants Need

1   Draw a picture of the best place to

2   Label your picture. Think about wha
    grow well. Here are some words to l

light, sunlight, warmth, soil, air, water, nutrients, space

Growing Plants

Explore where plants grow near your school.

1   Draw a picture of the places where plants are growing well.

2   Draw a picture of the places where plants are struggling to grow.

3   Compare your pictures.

Plants grow well here	Plants struggle to grow here

4   Where were the healthiest plants found?

5   What do these places have in common that is helping the plants to grow well?

Places For Plants

1   List everything a plant needs to grow.

_____

_____

_____

_____

_____

2   Carry out research to find out if plants can grow under
     water, in the desert or in very cold places such as
     the Arctic.

3   Write about your findings below.

_____

_____

_____

_____

_____

_____

Watering Plants

1   Describe what happens to a plant that has not been watered.

_____

_____

_____

2   Draw and explain how plants receive water.

Plant Watering – Investigate it!

Ia Plan and carry out your own investigation to find out how much water plants need to live and grow.

Ib Describe what you will do.

---

2 List the equipment you will need.

---

3 What will you change?

---

4 What will you keep the same?

---

5 Make a prediction. What do you think might happen? Explain your answer.

I think _____

because _____

Keep a record of your observations for the next seven days.

6 Create a bar chart to show your results.

7a Which amount of water is better for the growth of a plant, measured by height?

7b How do you know?

8a Can you give a plant too much water?

8b How do you know?

Root Bound Plants

Malika, Alena and Megan have just knocked a plant off the window sill and found this.

I think the plant needs more space. We should put it into a bigger pot.

I think the plant is healthy. It is alive and green.

I think we should plant it outside in the ground. Plants should not be kept in pots.

I   **What needs to be done to help the plant grow better? Give your reasons.**

I think _____

because _____

How much grass seed? Investigate it!

Design an investigation to discover how much grass seed is needed to grow the perfect patch of grass.

1   **What equipment will you need?**

_____

_____

_____

_____

2   **What variable will you change?**   _____

3   **What variables will you keep the same?**

_____

_____

_____

4   **What will you measure or observe?**

_____

5   **What do you predict will happen?**

_____

6 Record your results here.

7 Explain your results. How much grass seed is needed for the perfect patch?

Make a Hydroponics Vase

Make a hydroponics vase like this.

1 **Use pictures and words to record any changes to the onion.**

Week	Picture	Comments
1		
2		
3		

Week	Picture	Comments
4		
5		
6		

Soil

Different soils have different nutrients.

1 **Explore some different planting materials such as compost, clay and sand.**

Soil type	Is it sticky?	Can you roll it into a ball?	Does it crumble and break easily?

2 **Write below any further observation you have made about the different soils.**

_____

_____

_____

_____

Investigating Soils

Plan a test to help you to find out which is the best soil for growing radishes.

1   **What will you change?** _____

2   **What variables will you keep the same?**

_____

3   **How often will you water your seeds?** _____

4   **How often will you observe?** _____

5   **Design a way to record your results.**

Using Fertiliser

Fertilisers contain nutrients and minerals that plants need to grow well. Explore two different fertiliser labels.

General Purpose Fertiliser	
Total nitrogen	20%
Available phosphate	10%
Potash	20%
Magnesium	0.5%
Iron	0.5%

Garden Safe
All Purpose Natural Organic Fertiliser

Total nitrogen	5%
Available phosphate	3%
Potash	3%
Calcium	9%
Sulfur	7%
Magnesium	1%

1 **Compare the ingredients and list all those found in both fertilisers.**

2 **Why does a plant need potassium?**

3 **Research the minerals and nutrients on your list. Write why each is important to plant growth.**

Investigating Fertiliser

Investigate how much fertiliser will make radishes grow better.

1   Discuss with a partner what 'better' will mean. Will you look for bigger leaves, more leaves, greener leaves, bigger radishes or something else?

_____

2   Fill in the table. Decide how many fertiliser pellets you will put into each pot to make the radish seeds grow better.

Pot	Number of fertiliser pellets
1	0
2	
3	
4	

The variable you are changing is the amount of fertiliser.

3   List the variables you must keep the same.

_____

_____

Mystery Seeds

Class 3 would like to grow these seeds and need some help.
Use all your knowledge about what plants need to answer their questions below.

1 **Should we plant our seeds in clay, sand, water, compost or something else?**

2 **Why is the size of the pot important?**

3 **Describe where we should grow our plants and explain why.**

4 **How much water should we give the seeds each day?**

5 **What else can we use to help our plants grow?**